CHILDREN OF THE SWASTIKA

EILEEN HEYES

CHILDREN OF THE SWASTIKA

THE HITLER YOUTH

THE MILLBROOK PRESS
BROOKFIELD, CONNECTICUT

4071858

Special thanks are due to the staff of the Simon Wiesenthal Center, particularly Aaron Breitbart, senior researcher, and Carol Perl, research assistant. Their help was essential to the preparation of this book.

I also want to express my deep appreciation to those former members of the Hitler Youth who shared stories of their experiences. Those reminiscences gave the organization a human dimension for me.

E.H.

Map by Joe LeMonnier

Photographs courtesy of: The Bettmann Archive: pp. 9, 13, 37, 58; National Archives: pp. 19, 77; UPI/Bettmann: pp. 24, 27, 73, 81; AP/Wide World: pp. 31, 34, 43, 63; New York Public Library Picture Collection: p. 45; Bundesarchiv, Koblenz: pp. 47, 55, 65.

Library of Congress Cataloging-in-Publication Data
Heyes, Eileen.
Children of the swastika : the Hitler Youth / by Eileen Heyes.
p.   cm.
Includes bibliographical references and index.
Summary: Describes the Hitler Youth, the state-sponsored youth organization founded by the Nazi regime to train boys and girls ten and older to serve Hitler's government with unquestioning devotion.
ISBN 1-56294-237-9 (lib. bdg.)
1. Hitler-Jugend—Juvenile literature.   2. Youth—Germany—Societies and clubs—Juvenile literature.   3. National socialism—Societies, etc.—Juvenile literature.   [1. Hitler Youth.   2. National socialism.   3. Germany—Politics and government—1933–1945.] I. Title.
DD253.5.H48   1993
324.243'038—dc20   92-13204   CIP   AC

Published by The Millbrook Press
2 Old New Milford Road, Brookfield, Connecticut 06804

CONTENTS

CHAPTER ONE
HITLER'S WORLD

Faith is harder to shake than knowledge, love succumbs less to change than respect, hate is more enduring than aversion. Anyone who wants to win the broad masses must know the key that opens the door to their heart. Its name is not objectivity (read weakness), but will and power.

Adolf Hitler, *Mein Kampf*

Alfons Heck led about 180 teenage boys in a desperate effort to strengthen Germany's defenses against invading forces in June 1944. Heck and his Hitler Youth unit went to a tiny town near the Luxembourg border to dig trenches that would stop tanks and to operate anti-aircraft guns.

Heck decided to close the local school so his boys could live there. The principal did the unthinkable. He protested.

"This is illegal," the man yelled. "I can't allow this at all."

Heck was stunned.

"Throw this man out," he told his two deputies. "If he comes back, shoot him." It was the old man's good fortune that he did not come back. For Heck, sixteen years old and fanatically devoted to Hitler, would not have hesitated. He would have had the man shot.

How could a boy barely old enough to shave wield this kind of life-and-death power?

To understand the answer to that, you have to look inside Nazi Germany. There, boys and girls aged ten and older were expected to belong to the Hitler Youth, the state-sponsored organization that would train them to serve their country with unquestioning devotion. They were to be the material from which a new world would be forged.

And you have to get acquainted with one of the twentieth century's most notorious mass murderers: Adolf Hitler.

A Hitler Youth unit salutes Adolf Hitler while parading past Nazi headquarters in Nuremberg.

The Germany that allowed Hitler to become its dictator was far different from the prosperous, staunchly democratic Germany of today. After World War I, Germany was a nation in turmoil: wrecked by war, angry at the terms under which it had surrendered, and reluctantly taking a crack at democracy for the first time.

The Weimar Republic, as the new German democracy was known, was proclaimed on November 9, 1918. Its constitution, which was officially adopted in August 1919, guaranteed equality, justice, and personal freedom to all Germans.

But the new government was in trouble almost from the moment it was created because Germans seethed with bitterness over the Treaty of Versailles, which had ended the war. Under the treaty, Germany had to give back land it had taken from France, Belgium, Denmark, and Poland, and it had to accept responsibility for starting the war. It had to pay huge reparations (payments for war damage) in gold and products (coal, ships, lumber, and the like). Most infuriating of all, the treaty virtually disarmed Germany by strictly limiting the number of troops in the army and prohibiting the country from having planes or tanks. On June 28, 1919, with grave misgivings, German leaders signed the treaty.

Miserable times followed. The early 1920s saw hyperinflation of the German currency, the Reichsmark, and money lost its value with dizzying speed. People carried paper money in boxes and wheelbarrows. Savings and investments were wiped out, salaries became worthless, and people were going hungry.

The people blamed the Weimar government for these problems. While the idea of democracy had flourished in England and France in the seventeenth and eighteenth centuries, petty tyrants had ruled much of Germany. Thus, a strong democratic tradition had not taken root among the German people. Although the German economy seemed to be rebounding in the mid-1920s, the worldwide depression that began in 1929 would again bring hard times and discontent with the Weimar government. And bad times for the people meant opportunity for a forceful, charismatic politician who could exploit the nation's anger and its fears.

Adolf Hitler was that politician.

Born on April 20, 1889, in Braunau am Inn, Austria, Hitler was the son of a middle-ranking customs official. In early youth, he decided that he had no interest in following in his father's career footsteps. He fancied himself something of an artist and considered becoming an architect. But doing so would have required more schooling than Hitler wanted to plod through.

Instead, he became a self-taught student of politics, reading newspapers avidly. He developed his own cynical and, it turned out, accurate analysis of what it took to captivate a mass of people. He would later put these lessons into practice with stunning success.

He also developed early in life the twin racial views that would drive him: that Germans were a "master race" and should be united in a single country, and that Jews were the source of Germany's ills. Although Hitler was Austrian by birth (he did not become a German citizen until 1932), he considered himself a German and thought there should be no national border separating the German-speaking peoples of Austria and Germany. This was another idea he would put into action later.

Hitler went to Munich, Germany, in 1913. In August 1914 he got permission to serve in the German Army in World War I. An impassioned warrior, Hitler was wounded twice and was decorated for bravery. After the war, he settled in Munich and worked as an education officer for the army—a job in which he discovered that he had a talent for public speaking. It was through this job that he got his start in politics.

In September 1919 he was sent to look at a tiny political group called the German Workers' Party. He had never heard of it. But Hitler found that it espoused many of his views. He was startled when the group invited him to join, but he saw that he could quickly become the leader of this pathetic little band of misfits and mold the organization to his own will.

A powerful speaker and skillful organizer, Hitler began to build up the party. Early in 1920 the group changed its name to the National Socialist German Workers' Party (NSDAP, by its German initials)—the Nazi party, for short. That summer Hitler designed a party flag that featured the swastika, a symbol borrowed from ancient times.

As hard times gripped the nation in the early 1920s, Hitler thought he saw his opportunity to make a grab for power. On November 8, 1923, in what came to be called the Beer Hall Putsch, he managed to corner the three highest officials of the state of Bavaria in the back room of a Munich beer hall. He demanded a share of power. Hitler's putsch, or rebellion, turned into a fiasco and landed him in prison for treason in 1924. But it made Hitler a national figure and a hero in the eyes of many. He received a five-year sentence but served less than nine months—from April 1 to December 20, 1924.

When he got out of prison, Hitler returned to the task of pulling new members into the party; by 1929, membership stood at 178,000. More important, he organized an intricate party structure much like that of the government. Nationwide, the party was divided into districts, which were then subdivided into several levels of smaller groups

Hitler and a group of brownshirts, as his storm troopers were called, in Munich around 1930.

down to streets and blocks. The party had its own departments of agriculture, justice, labor, race and culture, engineering, and foreign affairs, in addition to a busy propaganda office. Hitler also set up party groups for women, students, teachers, civil servants, doctors, lawyers, and artists. The Hitler Youth was such a group, with its own departments of culture, schools, press, propaganda, and so on. All this early organizing was done because Hitler realized that, if and when he finally managed to overthrow the Weimar government, he would need to have something ready to take its place immediately.

With the worldwide depression that began in 1929, Hitler again saw that conditions were right for change. But this time he was determined to take power by legal means and *then* make his revolution. So while he wooed the voters with rallies and propaganda, he also courted the army, the president, and Germany's major businessmen.

The depression hit Germany hard. Banks and businesses failed, millions of people were thrown out of work, farmers could not make their mortgage payments, and young people wanted some prospect of a better future. Hitler offered solutions to Germany's problems. He promised to give people jobs, to cast off the shackles of the hated Treaty of Versailles, to restore national pride. But, most sinister of all, he offered a scapegoat, someone to blame for all that was wrong with the German Fatherland: the Jews.

Perhaps more than anything else, this is what history remembers about Hitler. Before he was finished, Hitler would order the murder of nearly six million Jews—the vast majority of them from outside Germany—in a government-sponsored killing spree that became known as the Holocaust.

No one foresaw this in the early 1930s. The Nazi party was growing steadily and made impressive showings in elections, but it *never won a majority of votes.* Still, the party's new clout led at last to Hitler's appointment as chancellor, the head of the German government, on January 30, 1933. He immediately began to solidify his control of the country. Nazi storm troopers—the Sturmabteilung, or SA—began to beat up and murder opponents. On February 27, 1933, the Berlin Parliament building, the Reichstag, was torched. The Nazis blamed the Communists, and within a day Hitler had persuaded the aging President Paul von Hindenburg to suspend civil liberties and put all power in the hands of the central government. Thousands were arrested. Many were tortured and beaten. It was the first taste the nation got of Nazi terrorism with government backing. It would not be the last.

The Reichstag had been set ablaze days before a scheduled parliamentary election, and the Nazi party mounted a massive campaign to whip up public fear of a Communist menace. But the Nazis still fell short of a majority in the Reichstag election of March 5—the last free election during Hitler's life.

It didn't matter. On March 23, 1933, the Reichstag passed an Enabling Act that effectively handed over dictatorial powers to Hitler. He now had the freedom to rule Germany according to his own maniacal and murderous whims—and, though he had never gained the support of a majority of voters, he had attained that deadly power by legal, constitutional means.

The brutal actions of the Nazis should have come as no surprise. Hitler had spelled out his program of racial hatred and world conquest in remarkable detail in his book *Mein Kampf* ("My Struggle"), published in 1925.

Hitler began writing the two-volume *Mein Kampf* while he was in prison after the Beer Hall Putsch. In it, he explained his view that Germans belonged to an Aryan "master race" and therefore had the right to rule over all "inferior" peoples. When Germans needed more "living space," or *Lebensraum*, they should simply take it from countries to the east, Hitler declared.

He went on at length about his revulsion for the Jews, whom he did not consider to be Germans. In an eerie hint at what was to come, he wrote: "The nationalization of our masses will succeed only when, aside from all the positive struggle for the soul of our people, their international poisoners are exterminated."

Hitler explained in detail how he planned to win the hearts and minds of the masses with oratory, how their enthusiasm could be harnessed for his purposes, and how violence could give power to his movement. He also pointed out that the people would be more easily bent to his will if he could focus the nation's hate and anger on a single enemy.

Sure enough, when he became chancellor of Germany in 1933, he put all those plans and ideas into action.

First, Hitler put Nazis in charge of all the state governments. All other political parties were crushed. Trade unions were dissolved. Judges were intimidated, and Nazi thugs were sent out to beat and kill whomever they chose without interference from the police. Hitler also issued laws barring Jews from public service, the universities, and the professions. On April 1, 1933, he proclaimed a national boycott of Jewish shops. Nazi book-burning began with a torchlight parade on May 10, 1933, when about 20,000 books were set ablaze in Berlin.

Next, Hitler secretly began to rebuild the German Army for war, and he pulled Germany out of the League of Nations. This followed exactly the plan he had laid out in *Mein Kampf.* But even as he was building up the army, Hitler preached world peace. On January 26, 1934, Germany and its neighbor Poland announced a ten-year non-aggression pact. The pact was a scam, as the Poles would later learn.

On August 2, 1934, with the death of President von Hindenburg, Hitler made himself Germany's supreme ruler. He jettisoned the title of president and declared himself to be *Fuehrer* (leader) and Reich chancellor. Hitler called his state the Third Reich: the first Reich, he said, had been the Holy Roman Empire of 962 to 1806, and the second had been Otto von Bismarck's reign from 1871 to 1890. Hitler declared that his Reich, or empire, would last a thousand years.

It may seem odd that Germans tolerated Hitler's

abuses of power. But at this point, he had the support of the army, whose officers had sworn an oath of loyalty to him, and the businessmen, who were making money rearming. For it was the rebuilding of the German war machine that was ending the hard economic times the nation had endured. The German people had lost their personal freedoms and were now living a very regimented life, but they had jobs and a new confidence in the future of their country.

Concentration camps had sprung up, but at first they were mainly places where Nazi thugs could haul prisoners and beat them. The early camps were intended to deter opponents of the Reich, but they took on a ghastly new role as Hitler moved against the Jews.

With the Nuremberg Laws of September 15, 1935, Hitler took German citizenship from the Jews and made them "subjects." They were forbidden to marry Aryans or to employ female Aryan servants of childbearing age. Jews were forced to sell their businesses dirt-cheap or give them to non-Jewish Germans. In October and November of 1938, thousands of Jews of Polish descent were rounded up in Germany and dumped across the border into Poland.

On the night of November 9, 1938, Nazis torched synagogues and smashed windows in Jewish homes and businesses throughout Germany in a burst of terror that became known as Kristallnacht, the "night of broken glass." More than 30,000 Jewish men between the ages of 18 and 65 were sent to concentration camps.

It was not until late January 1942 that Nazi leaders formalized their "Final Solution of the Jewish Problem": Jews from throughout Europe who were able to work would be sent to work camps (where, of course, they were meant to be worked to death); those who could not work would be killed immediately. For this task, the Nazis secretly set up six death camps, all in rural Poland.

When Hitler came to power in 1933, there were more than 500,000 Jews in Germany—less than one percent of the population. Most managed to get out of Germany. Many committed suicide. By 1941 only 164,000 remained. Of these, 125,000 eventually died in Nazi camps.

Almost four fifths of the 5.8 million* Jews killed came from Poland and other parts of Eastern Europe. Also marked for death in Nazi camps were the incurably sick (90,000 were killed), Gypsies (300,000 to 1 million killed), the Polish leading classes (3 million), and Russian prisoners of war (3 million).

Meanwhile, Hitler began to amass the living space he desired. With a combination of threats, ruthless bullying, and questionable diplomacy, he achieved a series of conquests without causing a drop of blood to be shed.

First, on March 7, 1936, German troops reoccupied the Rhineland in western Germany, which had been demilitarized since World War I. The French, Germany's neighbors to the west, did not resist. On January 30, 1937, Hitler officially proclaimed the Treaty of Versailles dead—which it had been in fact for some time.

Next, on March 13, 1938, after some shady diplomatic maneuvering, Germany's Anschluss, or annexation, of Austria was proclaimed. The Nazis sent in troops and declared Austria to be "a province of the German Reich."

---

* Historians disagree on the number of Jews killed by the Nazis. This figure, 5.8 million, is from the *Encyclopaedia Judaica* and is the most widely accepted estimate, according to Aaron Breitbart, senior researcher at the Simon Wiesenthal Center for Holocaust Studies in Los Angeles. Respected Holocaust scholar Raul Hilberg, in *The Destruction of the European Jews* (student edition, New York: Holmes & Meier, 1985), put the number at 5.1 million. Documents released from Soviet Union archives in 1989, however, suggest that Nazis killed a quarter-million more Jews than had previously been believed. Research continues.

A Czech woman sobs as she dutifully salutes the Nazi forces that carved up her country in 1938.

Next came Czechoslovakia. In the Sudetenland region of Czechoslovakia lived about 3.25 million ethnic Germans. Hitler wanted to annex the region, and he assured the leaders of Great Britain and France that this would be his last territorial demand. With their cooperation, Hitler carved up the hapless Czechoslovakia (which was given no choice in the matter), and by the middle of March 1939 the nation had ceased to exist.

That same month, Hitler took the port district of Memel in Lithuania. This was to be his last bloodless conquest.

On the home front, Hitler was also expanding his power. His SS—Schutzstaffel, or protection squad—began as a private guard and grew into a Nazi army and one of the most powerful organizations in the Third Reich. Its leader was the infamous Heinrich Himmler. A police unit in Prussia became an arm of the SS in 1934 and developed into a force whose name inspired terror inside and outside Germany. It was the secret state police, or Geheime Staatspolizei—the Gestapo.

Hitler kept control over his people. Some he held with their love of the Fatherland, some he captured with the power of their own hate, and the rest he paralyzed with fear.

But many Germans had their doubts about Hitler. They remembered the horrors of World War I, and they were repulsed by the Nazis' penchant for violence. As the 1933 election results had shown, many did not feel a true devotion to the Nazi party.

Hitler knew well that, if the Third Reich was to thrive, he needed a huge pool of dedicated Nazis who would follow him without question. The older generation could not be counted on to do this.

What he needed, Hitler knew, were the children.

CHAPTER TWO
A PLACE FOR
YOUTH

*I am beginning with the young. We older ones
are used up. . . . We are rotten to the marrow.
We have no unrestrained instincts left. . . .
But my magnificent youngsters! Are there
finer ones anywhere? . . . With them I can
make a new world.*

Adolf Hitler, 1933

The German youth movement was strong and dynamic long before a jobless Austrian named Adolf Hitler ever came to Munich. It began in the late nineteenth century and grew quickly after World War I into a large but incohesive collection of organizations that were political, paramilitary, religious, sports oriented, and then some.

Many young Germans at this time were in despair. Their nation was a shambles after the war. Their elders had delivered them a world with myriad problems and little promise of a brighter future. With the exuberance and untarnished idealism of youth, they were grasping for a way to get control of their lives and trying to forge a path to a stronger, prouder Germany.

It was against this backdrop of restlessness and longing for a better nation that the Hitler Youth came into being.

Hitler proclaimed the formation of the first Nazi youth group in March 1922, with a call for members in the party's newspaper. The notice stated outright that the Nazis wanted to form a pool of future party members, storm troopers (SA), and "fighters against the Jewish enemy." The group's statutes said the Germanic spirit would be nurtured by weekly meetings, lectures, hiking trips, and sports. Every second Sunday was to be spent hiking in the countryside.

In July 1926 the Hitler Youth was formally founded under the name Hitler Jugend, Bund Deutscher Arbeiterjugend (Hitler Youth, League of German Workers' Youth), with Kurt Gruber as its leader. About the same time, in an effort to gain support from as many segments of society as possible, the Nazi party founded groups for women, students, teachers, lawyers, and others.

The Hitler Youth at first was attached to the SA, and members wore brown shirts like those worn by the party storm troopers, plus an armband with a swastika. The group's main activities in the 1920s were spreading propaganda and doing publicity for the party. Party control over the Hitler Youth was weak throughout the 1920s, and the group actually managed to maintain some independence from Nazi domination. Many of its members and leaders truly believed in the "socialism" part of National Socialism. Hitler, of course, had little interest in socialist ideals—except when they could be used to further his political aims.

Gruber got Hitler's attention on August 19–20, 1927, when he led about three hundred youths participating in the annual national Nazi party rally in Nuremberg. Hitler paid tribute to the young men's dedication, and with this the group gained a secure place in the party. Less than two years later, in April 1929, the Hitler Youth was declared the only official youth group of the Nazi party, and a place was reserved for it at all future party rallies. A girls' section had been formed in 1927, but it got nowhere until it was formally named the League of German Girls (Bund Deutscher Maedel, or BDM) in July 1930. In 1932, it was made the only party group for girls.

Although there was not yet any regular, systematic indoctrination of young people, Hitler Youth members were encouraged to think of themselves as soldiers and missionaries. They were to fight to bring down the Weimar government, and they were to spread the Nazi gospel among their not-yet-believing peers.

In 1931 the party moved to tighten its grip on the growing youth group. The Hitler Youth was in disarray,

National youth director Baldur von Schirach receives the salutes of Hitler Youth members after delivering a radio address on the ideals of National Socialism.

district leaders' reports were shoddy and late, and dues were not getting paid to national headquarters on time. Gruber, who had proved incapable of running a national organization, was ousted. His replacement was Baldur von Schirach, twenty-four—a devoted follower of Hitler, a hard worker, and a good organizer. In his new position as national youth director, the baby-faced Schirach was just the person to turn the Hitler Youth into a powerful tool of the Nazi party.

The group set up leadership schools and planned camps to teach party ideology, racial theory, and other subjects. Members were expected to attend weekly *Heimabends*, or "home evenings," for informal political instruction and to plan the week's propaganda activities. Schirach purged the Hitler Youth of leaders who wanted to promote socialism and turned the group's attention to nationalism. Piece by piece, he was building a machine to turn out millions of loyal future Nazis.

Help came in 1932 from an unexpected source: the government. Nazi power was growing, and violence was the party's trademark. In an effort to stop the Nazi street fighting, the government banned a number of Nazi groups—including the Hitler Youth—on April 13, 1932. The ban lasted only a few months, but the forbidden group (temporarily using a different name) grew immensely in popularity. Recruits appeared in droves. By October of that year, Schirach was able to gather 80,000 youths in Potsdam for two days of speeches, marches, singing, and flag-waving. It showed the nation that Hitler, whom so many had dismissed as a has-been after the Beer Hall Putsch, had a huge and adoring mass of youngsters in the palm of his hand.

On the evening of January 30, 1933, when Hitler was hailed as the new chancellor, Hitler Youth columns marched with other Nazi party supporters in a wild celebration of power. From then on, the Hitler Youth became increasingly enslaved to the party. Its role now was to bring youths into the Nazi fold and take control of all aspects of young life. In less than a year, the more than four hundred other youth groups in Germany—except the Catholic groups, which were allowed to exist until 1937—were destroyed.

Hitler Youth leaders made no secret of their intention to turn out millions of dedicated young Nazis. During

1933, membership in Hitler Youth units skyrocketed from about 120,000 to almost 2.3 million. Within three years, that figure had doubled. But about half the nation's youth still had not been signed up. In December 1936 the Hitler Youth Law theoretically made membership compulsory; by the time the Reich began enforcing the law in 1939, eighty-two percent of eligible youths—7.3 million—already belonged. It was the largest youth organization in the world, and the task it set for itself was huge: the Hitler Youth meant to make a whole generation think and act in total, fanatical uniformity.

Its approach to this goal was stunningly comprehensive. Youths were drawn into police work, population resettlement, agriculture, racial policy, sports, the military, and concentration-camp operations. The SS, Hitler's elite police and military force, expressed an early interest in the Hitler Youth, and eventually turned the group into a source of recruits for its sinister and deadly projects. The Hitler Youth and the SS complemented each other as instruments of social control—the one molding the minds of the young, the other using terror to keep resisters in line.

The Reich's Land Service, on the other hand, had more benign aims—at least superficially. With the slogan of "Blood and Soil," the Nazi party called for urban citizens to return to the land. The Land Service, introduced on October 7, 1934, was part of this plan, and every member of the Hitler Youth and the BDM was required to participate. The service sent them to work on farms. The SS ultimately made this a source of recruits, too.

Soon after Hitler's ascension to power, all courses in the schools—from history to physics—were rewritten to fit Nazi racial and political doctrines. Competitive sports and physical training became central to the education of young Germans.

Young Hitler Youth members march through the streets of Nuremberg, which are decorated for a Nazi party rally.

Beginning at age six, a boy served a sort of apprenticeship in the Hitler Youth. From ages ten to fourteen, boys joined a unit called the Jungvolk (Young Folk) and girls went into the Jungmaedel (Young Girls). At fourteen, boys went into the Hitler Youth proper, girls into the BDM. When the war caused labor shortages, older teens were assigned through Hitler Youth programs to do various kinds of public service.

The Nazis were fond of declaring that youth should be led by youth, and most Hitler Youth leaders were in their twenties. Once again, Hitler shrewdly managed to bend a huge number of people to his will. For without supervisors and instructors who could remember life before the Nazis, the Hitler Youth grew up knowing no rule but that of National Socialism and no leader but Hitler. Not surprisingly, the young became the Fuehrer's most fanatically devoted followers.

Hitler recognized early on that the loyalty of youth would be crucial to his success. It is a subject he returned to many times in *Mein Kampf.* Physical training and the nurturing of strong, healthy bodies, he wrote, were of utmost importance. Schools should devote more time to this and stop burdening students with boring lessons that they would quickly forget anyway. Boys must grow into good soldiers, and girls must become good mothers and bear strong boys.

Such was Hitler's plan for fully exploiting the nation's youth. Although there was some dissent, the young people of Germany were largely captivated by the Nazi program. The Hitler Youth leaders demanded a lot from them, but in return they gave youths an almost irresistible package of rewards. They saw to it that youngsters were well fed, that they got a taste of power, and that they had a good time.

CHAPTER THREE
FUN, FUN,
FUN

This self-confidence must be inculcated in the young national comrade from childhood on. His whole education and training must be so ordered as to give him the conviction that he is absolutely superior to others. Through his physical strength and dexterity, he must recover his faith in the invincibility of his whole people.

Adolf Hitler, *Mein Kampf*

All things considered, life was good for young members of Hitler's master race. They were given extra food rations, hailed often by the Fuehrer himself, and kept busy with an array of activities that often seemed pure pleasure.

Hitler meant to create a youth state within a state. The Hitler Youth was to be the framework for young people's lives, and they were to have virtually no life outside it. With this in mind, youth leader Baldur von Schirach set up camps for every kind of activity. Teens in a camp could be easily supervised and controlled—even as they enjoyed the tents, cookouts, campfires, and field sports.

Physical training and cultural work were among the required activities in the Hitler Youth. Physical training was most important, for boys and girls alike. Although the youngsters were not told this, Hitler knew there was war ahead and wanted plenty of strong soldiers to send to battle. Hitler exhorted his young comrades to become "tough as leather, swift as greyhounds, hard as Krupp steel."

So sports and fitness were constantly emphasized. This was a stroke of genius: Young people have a natural drive to compete, to excel, to win. The Nazis tapped this rich vein of enthusiasm and involved millions of youths in track and field, gymnastics, hiking, war games, and marksmanship. Paraphernalia, pomp, and mysticism made some of the activities seem like religious rituals.

Everything was made into a competition—not only sports, but fund-raising, record keeping, music, storytelling, and cleanliness—to keep teenagers interested in

Members of a Hitler Youth unit carry full backpacks as they set out on a 1934 overnight march in Bavaria.

giving their all. The National Sports Competition drew 1.5 million participants in 1933, the year Hitler became chancellor, and by 1939 had grown to include 7 million. That year, nearly eighty percent of teenagers competed in these contests. There was also a yearly National Vocational Competition, which drew 3.5 million boys and girls in 1939.

Winning was not the only goal. Sports were also a means to teach how to lead and how to follow. Even everyday play was organized to give practice in the leader-follower relationship. The Hitler Youth urged young people to push themselves until they were nearly exhausted. The leaders knew that getting tired out while having fun with others would leave a strong bond of camaraderie. Obedience to leaders and loyalty to comrades would be crucial on the battlefield.

The organization reached into every corner of Germany. It set up youth centers and gymnastic facilities to help break down social walls between children of landowners and children of laborers. In farm areas, infant mortality was high, child labor was exploited, physical deformities were disproportionately common, and children got little education. The Hitler Youth provided exercise programs, medical and dental care, and showers in the schools.

Through Hitler Youth programs, many teens spent months at youth camps and also worked on farms or in private homes. Sports, singing or dancing, and discussions usually were part of every day—along with long hours of manual labor. For those who sought it, the Hitler Youth provided cultural outlets, such as youth choirs and music festivals. Girls would spend hours on art projects and crafts.

Following are some recollections of former members of the Hitler Youth and its affiliates. They illustrate the marked difference between the boys' and girls' training: While boys were heavily dosed with political propaganda, girls often escaped such blatant indoctrination completely. The boys, after all, were expected to grow up to be leaders. The girls, for the most part, needed only to know how to be good wives and mothers.

These are the voices of real people who now live in the United States; they told their stories for this book but wanted to remain anonymous. So powerful is Hitler's legacy that even half a century later and thousands of miles away from their homeland, they fear harassment because of their former association with the Third Reich.

"Heidi" has been in the United States since 1956. She lived in Nuremberg, the national center for sports competitions. She joined the Jungmaedel, the Young Girls, around 1939, before she was ten.

"We had meetings Wednesday and Friday afternoons," Heidi recalls. "On Wednesdays we were singing and talking. And then we were marching out in the fields. Friday was sports day." This meant field and track in summer, gymnastics in winter. "Every year, spring and fall, there were the big sports competitions at the big sports arenas. You had to participate."

Heidi was athletic and usually won her races. She never threw away the pins she was awarded for those victories.

Crafts were also part of the Wednesday meetings. "Usually for Christmas, we were involved in lots of art, especially for children. We made little stuffed animals and toy boxes. And before Christmas we had a big exhibition, and again you were competing with all the other groups. And you always got a little reward if you were the best, or you had the most or the most beautiful." They gave the toys to needy children.

BDM girls perform a folk dance at
a 1933 Hitler Youth rally.

"In the summertime on Wednesdays, we went out in the field and we picked herbs for the pharmacies, mostly to make tea. And again, you got a reward when you were the winning group. There was always a competition."

She joined the Jungmaedel, with her parents' blessing, because "it was an honor to go. So almost everybody went. Unless you were weak or sick or [a] Jew or something; then, of course, they didn't want you."

The Jungmaedel training camps, she recalls, were "fun and tough. I was always hungry. And at those camps, they trained you for survival, on a little tiny bit of food. One day, I discovered all the food in the kitchen. And I went to our leader and I questioned why we wouldn't get anything to eat." The leader promised to take her question higher, and that night at dinner the girls were asked "Who is hungry?" Heidi stood up and urged some of her friends to follow suit. "That night, we didn't get anything to eat, and all the next day. From that time on, I never opened my mouth."

Heidi has no regrets about being in the Jungmaedel. "I was in it with all my heart," she remembers, "because we did nothing but good."

"Karl" grew up in Nuremberg. He joined the Jungvolk at age ten, shortly before the war started. He came to the United States in the early 1950s and is now a U.S. citizen.

"Most children the same age were a member of that group," Karl remembers. "If there's a group of Boy Scouts in your neighborhood, you want to become a member, too. We were looking forward to going to meetings, because we had a sense of belonging that everybody wants to have. Many times, it was just fun to be there.

"There were two meetings, normally on Wednesday and Friday. At first there were history lectures that were about the ancient Norwegians and Germans. There was a bit of marching. We were eager to learn. Everything looked rosy. To die for the Fatherland sounded really great.

"At the camps were a lot of games. The games were most of the time oriented toward paramilitary training. 'Trapper and Indian' was the only thing you might have wanted to play. But it was soldiering. It was exercises on how to conceal yourself in the country, how to attack enemies. Everyone wanted to go, because it was a way to get away from school and to have some fun. There were a lot of parades. It just was a promotion of the patriotic spirit. And most everybody wanted to go along with that because they still didn't realize what the ultimate goal of the leadership was."

Nazi indoctrination was nonstop. "Exercises, lectures in history, political lectures, the purity of the Aryan race—a lot of what in later life you think is garbage. There were a lot of good things in it. And a lot of nonsense that the political people were trying to brainwash you with.

"The main thing that stuck with me is that there is no country that is any better than the others. For a lot of years, I had a guilt complex, because of things that happened in Germany during the war. But now I know these things can happen just as well in this country."

"Elizabeth" joined the Jungmaedel in 1939 at age ten, over the objections of her grandfather. After the war she married an American serviceman and came to the United States. She became a U.S. citizen in the mid-1950s.

"Everybody that I knew was in there, and they all had a good time participating in sports events. And then, of course, we went hiking and camping. I was an only child. And to me, it was the friendship that developed and the comradeship, because I really didn't have anybody to play with. So I enjoyed going on the hiking trips and doing things together in groups and marching and singing.

"Before the war started, we went in the summer for a week at a time to camp. We would roam around in the woods, pick berries, and sit around a campfire and play games. It was fun. And, of course, we got into all the mischief that everybody would get into at our age. I guess at that age you don't comprehend the seriousness of it. But as far as I'm concerned, in the Hitler Youth, you did learn discipline. That stands out with me. I remember that."

A Hitler Youth drum corps. Patriotic parades were one of the group's major attractions for young people.

Because her grandfather, the family patriarch, objected to her joining the Hitler Youth, Elizabeth had to be careful not to bring anything home from the group and to keep her enthusiasm to herself.

"I was allowed to join," she recalls, "but not to be too ambitious, not become a leader. And everybody wanted to be a leader. You had more say-so over the other kids."

She doesn't remember having any awareness of the concentration camps. "There were a lot of people that were defiant of the party that they would pick up and bring somewhere, but we had no idea where or to what. Of course, at my age I didn't understand, or didn't care, or didn't know what it was all about."

"Johann" was the son of a German businessman in Kobe, Japan. He joined the Hitler Youth there at age ten, shortly before Germany went to war. He came to the United States in 1949 and became a U.S. citizen about 1955.

"My father was in the export-import business and had lived in Japan for quite a while," he remembers. "There was a foreign community of a few thousand in Kobe." A local branch of the Hitler Youth was formed for the sons and daughters of Germans in Kobe. Johann and his older sister joined.

"Like all kids at that age, you had to join because all your friends did. During the war, it became very important [to belong], because when food became scarce and food rationing set in, it was a wonderful way to punish people, by simply not giving them rations: 'If you're not willing to do your share by joining the Hitler Youth, you don't deserve to eat.'

"When I was ten, none of these considerations mattered. What really was the motivation for a lot of people was that it was a lot of fun. There was always a two- or three-week summer camp. In the winter there was always a ski trip for one or two weeks. When you're young, you hardly know what's going on. It's only later on that you realize that there were subtle pressures and subtle indoctrinations taking place."

Johann's father wasn't fooled, though.

"My father was never a party member. Hitler came to power in 1933, and we left just before that and we never went back because my father did not like what was going on in Germany. Now that it's been almost fifty years since all that happened, one can look back and say it's hard to believe it really happened. It's a world that's so different that you can't really reconstruct it in your own memory."

"Gertrud" lived in a suburb near Cologne. She was eight when Hitler became chancellor, and she joined the Jungmaedel at eleven or twelve, around 1936. She came to the United States in 1954 and became a U.S. citizen in 1959.

"My parents tried to keep me out as long as they could. I wanted to join earlier, but my dad wouldn't let me. All my friends were in there, too. I experienced almost no political indoctrination. There were a lot of sports—which I hated because I was very poorly coordinated, and I tried to get out of it as often as I could. I was always the last one chosen to be on a team, and the last one in a run. I experienced it as very harmless. I don't even think that a word was ever said against the Jews.

"There were a lot of patriotic songs. And there was a flag raising every morning. Well, we have that here, too. Once a week, it would be either sports or outings. We were involved once or twice a year in some fund-raising for the welfare programs." At meetings, she would read, play games, or make crafts.

"You were enthusiastic about the activities, about belonging with your peers. You really didn't understand anything about the party at that age."

Looking back, Gertrud thinks of the Jungmaedel as something that was a bit annoying because she didn't like sports and resented the strict meeting schedule. Still, she says:

"I at the time didn't see anything wrong with it. And in retrospect, I also don't see anything wrong with it. If I saw anything wrong with that, I would have to see just as much wrong with pledging allegiance to the flag and going to the Boy Scouts or Girl Scouts."

Young people in Hitler's Germany learned many real virtues. They learned courage, loyalty, and discipline. In the process, though, they missed out on one vital lesson of growing up. They never learned to question authority.

The Nazi effort to produce a generation of strong, agile bodies was quite successful. And amid all the attention given to physical training, Hitler Youth leaders did not for a minute neglect their other task: the training and manipulating of young minds.

CHAPTER FOUR
FROM FUN TO
FANATICISM

*Above all we appeal to the mighty army of our
German youth. They are growing up at a great
turning point and the evils brought about by
the inertia and indifference of their fathers will
force them into struggle. Some day the German
youth will either be the builder of a new folkish
state, or they will be the last witness of total
collapse, the end of the bourgeois world.*

Adolf Hitler, *Mein Kampf*

The day was September 10, 1938; the place, Nuremberg. This was the Day of the Hitler Youth at the annual Nazi party rally. Young people from throughout Germany marched into the city stadium and performed maneuvers they had practiced for a year in their home districts. The drills were perfect, a masterpiece of planning.

Just before noon, 80,000 boys and girls lined up in the stadium. They stood at parade rest, tingling with anticipation. The youths endured a speech by Baldur von Schirach, the national youth leader. But this was not what they were there for. They wanted to see their leader.

Finally, Adolf Hitler appeared.

The children thundered: *"Sieg Heil! Sieg Heil! Sieg Heil!"* Hail victory!

Hitler began quietly, as usual. He steadily increased his volume and tempo, then slowed again, only to build to the next peak. It was a technique that held listeners spellbound. At last, his voice rising and his fist jabbing the air, the Fuehrer shouted:

"You, my youth, are our nation's most precious guarantee for a great future, and you are destined to be the leaders of a glorious new order under the supremacy of National Socialism. Never forget that one day you will rule the world!"

The assembly erupted into a frenzy. Near-hysterical youths shouted *"Sieg Heil!"* for several minutes. Many were in tears. Their bodies, their minds, and their hearts belonged to Adolf Hitler.

Such was the control that Hitler, a master at manipulating people, wielded over German youths. It was no

Tens of thousands of Hitler Youth members fill the Nuremberg stadium to hear Hitler speak.

accident. While young people enjoyed the hiking, camping, singing, and camaraderie of the Hitler Youth, Nazi leaders were very deliberately molding them into obedient servants of the Third Reich.

Systematic indoctrination began in 1933, soon after Hitler became chancellor. Baldur von Schirach, who had been youth leader of the Nazi party since 1931, was named youth leader of the German Reich in June 1933. That year, virtually all other youth groups were banned and their members absorbed in a program called "coordination."

The Hitler Youth was no longer the youth branch of a political party, but the official youth organization of the Reich. It had to stop agitating against the government—as it had done in the Weimar years—and turn instead to instructing young people in the ideals of National Socialism and teaching that all activity should benefit the state.

Hitler Youth leaders set up an elaborate press and propaganda network with its own newspapers, movies, plays, and radio shows. At first, instruction was political. Gradually, though, it took on the tone of an almost mystical doctrine. Among the "prayers" children were required to memorize was this one: "Adolf Hitler, you are our great Fuehrer. Thy name makes the enemy tremble. Thy Third Reich comes, thy will alone is law upon earth. Let us hear daily thy voice and order us by thy leadership, for we will obey to the end and even with our lives. We praise thee! Heil Hitler!"

The sometimes subtle promotion of Nazi dogma was part of every Hitler Youth activity. Hiking, camping, sports, and other "fun" pursuits had their political purpose, and physical fitness was considered preparation for service to the Fatherland.

Public schools, from first grade through university, were put into the hands of Bernhard Rust, Reich minister

A page from a German children's book published during the Nazi years. Textbooks were rewritten and stories were revised to glorify Hitler and his party.

of education. Before Hitler took power, Rust had been fired from a teaching job for apparently being of unstable mind. He was devoted to Hitler. Under his leadership, schools were quickly Nazified.

Textbooks were rewritten to reflect Nazi racist views of the world, and *Mein Kampf* was made the "guiding star" of educators. Teachers had to join the Nazi Teachers League and promote Nazi doctrine in the classroom. Day after day, from the beginning of school, children were reminded how Hitler had restored Germany's dignity and cast off the shackles of the Treaty of Versailles.

Special schools were set up to train the elite, who were expected to become the next generation of Nazi leaders. The most important criteria for admission were good health, acceptable racial background, good character, and sufficient dedication to Hitler. For promising boys from poor families, fees were usually waived.

The National Political Educational Institutes—called Napola, a shortening of their German name—were founded in 1933. They were run by the education ministry as part of the long-established school system and were designed to produce leaders in all fields of German life, especially the military. Some of the Napola specialized in the humanities, others in natural sciences and foreign languages. A typical schoolday began at 8 A.M. with two hours of academics. Then came three hours of sports, then more academics, followed by art, music, or sports. Students were required to work in the surrounding community, on farms, or in factories, foundries, or coal mines. The Napola were kept somewhat independent of the party.

Not so the Adolf Hitler Schools. These were formally founded in 1937 as places to train future leaders of the Nazi party. They were under the direction of the Hitler Youth, outside the regular education system, and completely under party control. Local party leaders chose boys ages twelve to eighteen who were especially fanatical to send to the Adolf Hitler Schools. Academic subjects were treated lightly; emphasis was placed on sports and paramilitary training. During vacations, students were sometimes sent to party administrative offices to gain experience. (Similar schools were set up for girls, but in male-dominated Nazi society, the girls' schools taught almost nothing.) Adolf Hitler School graduates were supposed to attend a sort of finishing school for party leaders, the Nazi Order Castles. It took party leaders several years

Paramilitary training and political indoctrination were stressed in classes for future party leaders.

to decide on a three-year program for the Order Castles; then, in 1939, the outbreak of war put these schools out of business. Thus no students ever completed the entire three-year course.

Together, the schools sought to wipe out individualism and replace it with utter, unquestioning devotion to Germany. Lest any thought of God get in the way, the Hitler Youth strove to make Nazism the only religion of its members. Sunday parades were purposely scheduled at the same time as Catholic Masses. The annual Nazi rally in Nuremberg swept up young and old alike in its air of mystical religious fervor. A uniform ceremony for the swearing-in of fourteen-year-olds was meant to be a substitute for religious coming-of-age rites. Each summer saw a Day of the State Youth, another Nazi holiday that was added to the calendar as religious holidays were gradually dropped.

Beginning in the winter of 1935, the Hitler Youth and the SS took turns staging a solstice festival of pagan rituals in mountain or woodland settings. The programs included torchlight marches, songs, chanting, speeches, torch passing, games, and dancing by BDM girls. The ceremonies reflected SS chief Heinrich Himmler's obsession with wiping out Christian celebrations and replacing them with Nazi worship events.

Not all the Nazi propaganda was eagerly lapped up. Films produced by the National Youth Directorate were known to be horribly boring, and Hitler Youth members had to be forced to attend them. And when the *Hitler Youth Catechism* was published, the book was so unpopular that the leadership had a hard time giving copies away. But to openly defy the Nazi code could be dangerous.

The Hitler Youth created its own band of conformity enforcers called the Streifendienst, or Patrol Service, which worked closely with police. It was assigned to root out any deviation from the Nazi moral and ideological code. In 1938 it was charged with watching over all youths, not just Hitler Youth members. It became a sort of junior Gestapo.

What kind of offenses was the Patrol Service looking for? Smoking, drinking, improper saluting, curfew violations, singing of prohibited songs, disorderly conduct in billiard halls and dance halls, and similar strayings.

Schirach wanted the Patrol Service to enforce the same kind of social control within the Hitler Youth that the SS enforced within the Nazi party. These tasks included racial indoctrination and suppression of dissent, disloyalty, and nonconformity. The SS adopted it as a feeder organization.

After the war began, Reinhard Heydrich, chief of the Central Security Agency, figured out that the Patrol Service was a fine training ground for secret agents and domestic spies. In the summer of 1939, his agency began holding workshops for Patrol Service leaders. The youngsters were fascinated by the prospect of spying. They were pulled out of school for "auxiliary police work," and the training project was kept a secret. The security agency misled reluctant parents to get their permission. Heydrich didn't want to tell the public that he was recruiting teenage secret police agents. Within two months, more than two hundred boys between seventeen and twenty-one had been signed up. BDM girls were also recruited by the secret police, but mostly for office work.

Once the war began, churches tried to woo young people back. The Patrol Service was sent to spy on the churches. This tactic had the double effect of keeping tabs on the clergy and ensuring that children thought of the church as an enemy.

But the Patrol Service was not entirely successful in wiping out juvenile crime and rebelliousness. During the war, the Hitler Youth was plagued by "wild cliques," gangs of young rebels who dressed and acted like the gangsters they had seen in American and British movies. Himmler ordered that these teens be rounded up and sent to "protective custody camps." From there, the lucky ones were sent to the army or put to work for the government. The rest went to insane asylums, hospitals, or concentration camps. Some were sterilized. Others were "shot while trying to escape," a favorite Nazi way to get rid of troublemakers.

In the Nazi world, homosexuality was also considered a serious crime. Some youths who had homosexual experiences in their teens were later castrated or executed. The Hitler Youth itself was suspected of being a hothouse of homosexual activity.

The parents of all these youngsters were not blind, nor were they silent about the Nazi exploitation of youth. Some complained because their daughters came home from BDM/Hitler Youth camps pregnant. But their protests got them nowhere. Parents who failed to register a ten-year-old for the Hitler Youth could be fined or sent to prison. While the Reich talked about the ideal of the German family, it nurtured conflict between generations.

Youth leaders distributed questionnaires to secondary-school students, asking them to list anything parents, teachers, or employers had done to interfere with their Hitler Youth duties. When a Hitler Youth member was being considered for promotion, it sometimes helped his chances if his parents were anti-Nazi. For example, Walter Hess, a member in Wittlich, near the French border, made a name for himself when he turned in his father for calling Hitler a crazed Nazi maniac. The father landed in "protective custody." Walter was promoted.

Indeed, reporting remarks against the Fatherland or the Fuehrer was part of the standard instruction in the Hitler Youth. A person who stated that Germany should surrender could earn a death sentence as early as 1941. After some of Hitler's closest aides tried to kill him in 1944, such a remark was certain suicide. The older generations learned the hard way to watch what they said around the single-mindedly fanatical Hitler Youths.

Why were young people so loyal to Hitler?

There was more to the Nazi youth program than forcing political lessons down young throats and jailing anyone who disagreed. Hitler won the hearts of youths by promising a new world much better than the one they had been born into—something that young people every-where, at all times in history, have longed for.

The ideal was called *Volksgemeinschaft*, or National Community. Melita Maschmann, a BDM leader who was fifteen when Hitler came to power, recalls in her memoir *Account Rendered*: "What held my allegiance to this ideal-istic fantasy was the hope that a state of affairs could be created in which people of all classes would live together like brothers and sisters."

At an age when youngsters are often made to feel that they do not count, she and her peers were put into march-ing columns and told that they *did* count. The thought was intoxicating. This, Maschmann writes, was the Hitler Youth's appeal: "I wanted to escape from my childish, narrow life and I wanted to attach myself to something that was great and fundamental. This longing I shared with countless others of my contemporaries."

The Hitler Youth's most famous anthem ended with the line, "Today Germany listens to us, and tomorrow the whole world." But enthusiastic youths usually altered the German slightly and sang it as: "Today Germany belongs to us, and tomorrow the whole world."

■ 51 ■

The removal of the Jews did not go unnoticed. But in their devotion to the Fuehrer, young people accepted the explanation that Jews were simply being "deported." The government railed against a dark, evil "international Jewry" that it said was out to destroy Germany. Even though this did not seem to have any connection with the Jewish friends and neighbors they knew personally, youngsters had such strong faith in Hitler that they believed he must be doing the right thing.

Gertrud, who was only eight when Hitler took over, decades later recalled when the Jews were taken from Cologne, the nearest big city to her home. "My father came home from work and he said, 'They are rounding up the Jews and they are going to be sent to an internment camp.' At that point, we knew that they were being sent *somewhere*. But we didn't know that they were being sent to extermination." In fact, beginning in 1936, hundreds of seventeen-year-old boys volunteered for one-year terms in the SS Death's Head Formations, which guarded the concentration camps. Probably few understood when they volunteered that they would be involving themselves in genocide.

Melita Maschmann, long after Hitler's demise, tried to explain to a friend's teenage daughter how she and others had fallen for the Fuehrer: "We dreamed then of a strong Germany, respected amongst the nations not from fear but from admiration—and Hitler promised to fulfill this dream for us. Dreams are something dangerous in politics. They stop the dreamer from seeing what is really happening. Hitler whipped up our yearning political dream into a fanatical passion. When he had succeeded in doing this we followed him blindly. . . . In this state of bondage we had forfeited our freedom of conscience."

CHAPTER FIVE
A JUNIOR
ARMY

Give the German nation six million bodies with flawless athletic training, all glowing with fanatical love of their country and inculcated with the highest offensive spirit, and a national state will, in less than two years if necessary, have created an army.

Adolf Hitler, *Mein Kampf*

In Hitler's Germany, boys at age ten began to get ready for war. By the time they reached draft age, they were superbly fit, disciplined, and devoted. It wasn't enough just to love the Fatherland: You had to be willing to fight and, if need be, to die for it.

Ten-year-olds being sworn into the Jungvolk had to take this oath: "In the presence of this blood banner, which represents our Fuehrer, I swear to devote all my energies and my strength to the savior of our country, Adolf Hitler. I am willing and ready to give up my life for him, so help me God."

Imagine a fifth-grader making a commitment like that!

With physical training, ideological indoctrination, and Nazified education, the leaders of the Third Reich prepared young bodies and minds for the work of soldiering. To complete the picture, the Hitler Youth was organized like the Wehrmacht, the German army, with similar units and an iron chain of command.

The smallest unit was the Kameradschaft, with ten to fifteen boys. Other units were:

Schar: 3–4 Kameradschaften (50–60 boys)
Gefolgschaft: 3–4 Scharen (150–190 boys)
Unterbann: 4–6 Gefolgschaften (600–800 boys)
Bann: 5 or more Unterbanne

The 223 Banne, in turn, were collected into 42 Gebiete (each with around 75,000 boys), which made up the six Obergebiete (about 375,000 boys each).

*A poster promoting the League of German Girls
proclaims, "All ten-year-olds to us."*

The Gefolgschaft, something like a military company, was the most important unit. Each member was taught to think of his Gefolgschaft as his home and to give it his unwavering loyalty. To enhance this feeling among members, each Gefolgschaft had its own flag.

What made it all work was the Fuehrerprinzip, or leadership principle. Hitler harps on this again and again in *Mein Kampf.* The leadership principle worked in this way: Every leader at every level had almost unlimited authority over those in his command; he had the right to expect unquestioning obedience. But along with this, he bore responsibility for everything that happened in his unit. If someone in the group caused trouble, it was the group leader who paid the consequences.

Alfons Heck became an acting Bann leader (roughly the equivalent of a major-general in the U.S. Army) in the last months of the war; he was not quite seventeen. In his memoir *A Child of Hitler*, Heck recalls an incident early in his Hitler Youth career when his group leader marched all 160 boys in his unit into an ice-cold river in November. The reason: The group leader didn't like the way they sang. The boys grumbled, but not one refused. It would have been unthinkable.

Rising from the ranks into a leadership job in the Hitler Youth was a matter of merit. Generally speaking, all boys had an equal chance for promotion, no matter what their family background. The camps, sports, and premilitary training erased many social distinctions, and boys of all classes learned to work together and rely on each other. Some parents complained about this mixing of the classes, but that made it all the more appealing to youths who already felt alienated from their elders.

The girls' branch, the League of German Girls, or BDM, was organized very much like the boys' part of the

Hitler Youth. The smallest unit was the Maedelschaft (about fifteen girls). Other units and their sizes were approximately as follows:

Maedelschar: 3 Maedelschaften (50 girls)
Maedelgruppe: 3 Maedelscharen (150 girls)
Maedelring: 4 Maedelgruppe (600 girls)
Untergau: 5 Maedelring (3,000 girls)
Gau: 5 Untergaue (15,000 girls)
Obergau: 5 Gaue (75,000 girls)
Gauverband: 5 Obergaue (375,000 girls)

The Gauverband was the equivalent of the boys' Obergebiet.

But girls had a much different role in the world Hitler was trying to create. Although girls went through the same kind of sports training as boys, with the same emphasis on competitiveness, they were taught that they must grow up to be strong mothers and obedient wives. Their noblest duty, they were told, was to produce flawless children for the Fatherland. Equal opportunity did not extend to females in the Third Reich.

As Hitler states bluntly in *Mein Kampf*: "The goal of female education must invariably be the future mother." He goes on to say that the German girl "is a subject and only becomes a citizen when she marries." The Hitler Youth motto for girls was: "Be Faithful, Be Pure, Be German!" For boys, it was: "Live Faithfully, Fight Bravely, and Die Laughing!"

Boys in the Jungvolk learned semaphore reading, bicycle repairs, laying of telephone wires, and small-arms use. This latter included training with dummy hand grenades, air guns, and small-bore rifles.

When they graduated at age fourteen into the Hitler Youth proper, they had several options, besides the general

Members of a Hitler Youth Marine unit.
The Marine section was especially popular
in the north, near the coast.

Hitler Youth. In the Motor Hitler Youth, which at its peak had about 102,000 members, boys could learn vehicle mechanics and driving. The Marine section was especially popular in the north, where Germany has a coast, and its membership reached 62,000; in it, boys studied boating and navigation. Marine members helped ferry troops across the Rhine River during the war.

The elite were in the Flying Hitler Youth, where boys learned to fly gliders in preparation for air force service. After an initial three-week training session, they could take more advanced courses to attain higher flight ratings. The Flying Hitler Youth eventually had 78,000 members. In a small Signal section, boys learned communications. There was also a small Equestrian unit, designed to attract rural youths, which was concerned mainly with equestrian sporting events.

Disabled youths of acceptable racial background were also allowed to join the Hitler Youth, although they were not involved in military training. Instead, they were provided with recreation and instruction within their abilities, learning things like carpentry and clerical work.

At age eighteen, boys and girls were expected to serve for some months—the required age and length of service were changed several times—in the Reich Labor Service. Boys did manual and agricultural work and helped build bridges and roads. Afterward, they were immediately drafted into the army. Girls in the Labor Service were assigned to work in agriculture or in homes.

Hitler long ago had thought through the many meanings of military service. Besides the obvious purpose of waging war, the military could also be a powerful way to unite people into a mob when they might otherwise harbor dangerous individualistic ideas.

"What other peoples still primitively possess in their herd community instinct," he wrote in *Mein Kampf*, "we, partially at least, regained artificially for our national community through the process of military training." This is precisely how the Hitler Youth worked on young Germans. It turned them into a herd that could be led and, when the need arose, stampeded. In the game of manipulating people, Hitler played all the angles. And he was under no illusions about what his conquests would cost the youth of Germany. The price would be high, and it would have to be paid in blood. Hitler had no qualms about this.

In *Mein Kampf*—written, remember, in 1925, fourteen years before he started World War II—Hitler stated that the Nazis must do whatever they had to do "to secure for the German people the land and soil to which they are entitled on this earth." For this, he was perfectly willing to order "the investment of the sons of today." The glory of conquest, then, would "some day acquit the responsible statesmen of blood-guilt and sacrifice of the people."

So it was that, by the time the war began in 1939, the nation's youth had been fully prepared. Their bodies were fit. Their minds were filled with Nazi ideas. Their hearts belonged to the Fuehrer. And they were organized into the young equivalent of an army.

An entire nation of young people was ready to go to war.

CHAPTER SIX
WAR

None of us who reached high rank in the Hitler Youth will ever totally shake the legacy of the Fuehrer. Despite our monstrous sacrifice and the appalling misuse of our idealism, there will always be the memory of unsurpassed power, the intoxication of fanfares and flags proclaiming our new age.

Alfons Heck, *A Child of Hitler*

On September 1, 1939, the tanks of Hitler's Wehrmacht rolled into Poland while German warplanes roared overhead. World War II had begun.

Now all the years of training young people, of whipping up their fierce loyalty to the Reich, began paying off. The Hitler Youth was ready to fight and ready to do the real work of imposing Hitler's repopulation plan on Europe, by force if necessary.

Hitler Youth boys had spent years learning to use weapons, to fly gliders, and to maintain strict discipline: They were an ideal pool to draw soldiers and air force pilots from, and all branches of the military competed to recruit them. In the first month of the war, most Hitler Youth leaders of draft age went to the army or the Waffen-SS, the military arm of the SS.

By the year the war started, 1939, the Hitler Youth had 20,000 marksmanship teachers, including some sent from the army. More than 50,000 boys had earned the Marksmanship Medal, which required near-perfect shooting, while standing or lying down, at a distance of 50 meters (164 feet).

In fall of 1940 the National Youth Directorate called for sports, target practice, and terrain maneuvers for children ten and older. Even with the demands of the war, which was pulling many trainers onto the battlefield, about half a million boys got premilitary training in 1940 and 1941.

The next year, the Reich got serious about it. On March 13, 1942, Hitler decreed the creation of Military Training Camps (Wehrertuechtigungslager, or WELs) to

A boy practices for the Hitler Youth Marksmanship Medal. By late 1943, nearly all boys of seventeen were receiving premilitary training.

give three weeks of intensive training and indoctrination to all boys between sixteen and eighteen. The people who ran these camps wanted to fire up the teens' enthusiasm for the cause, so they tried to play down the military purposes and to nurture mental readiness and physical health.

The WELs began their work on May 10, 1942. By the end of 1943, nearly every boy of seventeen was getting premilitary training in one of the Hitler Youth's 226 WELs. The SS, ever in search of good young candidates, operated several dozen of the camps, which served as SS recruiting stations.

Every hour of the three-week WEL program was supervised, and ideological indoctrination was woven into every activity. Each week had a theme: "We Fight," teaching that war is part of nature's plan; "We Sacrifice," stressing total commitment to the cause; and "We Triumph," proclaiming that the ultimate good was the glory of Greater Germany. WELs taught that teamwork, orderliness, and cleanliness were the virtues of a good soldier. They also hammered at discipline and unquestioning obedience. The camps produced excellent soldiers and officer candidates.

Another war program that made the most of youths' dedication was the Land Service. Perhaps looking to avoid the draft, about 25,000 youngsters volunteered for the Land Service by mid-1939. When the war came, they too were forced into military uniforms, mostly with the Waffen-SS.

Still, the Land Service took on new significance in 1939 with the acquisition of Poland, which surrendered within a month after the Germans invaded. Hitler selected the captured parts of Poland to experiment with population transfers and his racial policy known as "Germanization." The idea was to make Poland into a new frontier

Nazi troops confront Polish refugees.
Polish farmers were turned off their land
to make room for German families.

where the prized Aryan race could multiply and thrive. And the people who would get that process started were the children—primarily the girls—of the Hitler Youth.

Each spring, youths, many of them unemployed, were plucked from the crowded cities and handed over to farmers. The "Blood and Soil" enthusiasts wanted to reverse the migration of young people from rural areas to the cities. They intended that youngsters in the Land Service should stay on the land, start good German families, and become farmers themselves. Expanding on this idea, Hitler ordered Heinrich Himmler, chief of the SS, to kick the "inferior" Polish farmers off their land and hand the farms over to German nationals and ethnic Germans from other conquered territories. Himmler and Artur Axmann, who succeeded Baldur von Schirach in 1940, planned for the Hitler Youth Land Service to play a major role in accomplishing this. Idealistic youngsters of the Hitler Youth were thoroughly convinced that it was the right thing to do for the good of the Fatherland.

In 1940 about 1,400 girls from the BDM, under the auspices of the Hitler Youth's Eastern Action and the Land Service, went east to help the new immigrants get settled. Many of the immigrants were ignorant of modern medicine and farming techniques. Girls of fifteen to twenty-one worked hard on the farms and in the villages. They harvested crops, cleaned houses, cared for babies, tended animals, taught the women to cook and sew, told German stories, sang folk songs, and gave German language instruction. They also staged plays, festivals, and cultural events to win the peasants' loyalty to the new Greater Germany.

Some elementary school teachers from the BDM went to the new territories to teach immigrant children. Other teachers were sent to rural areas of Germany, where the Hitler Youth ran camps for the hundreds of thousands of children evacuated from cities that the Allies were bombing.

BDM groups were founded in sixty-four settler villages, and they became a key force in each community. Settlers who at first were suspicious of the girls came to respect them for the long hours of hard work they did to back up their lofty talk of a new world. The girls also took on such jobs as performing weddings and baptisms, settling disputes, and providing health care. In the schools, they conducted sports training, taught music, and helped with homework.

The success of the Third Reich's population policy depended on the efforts of the Hitler Youth. While bureaucrats in faraway offices shuffled papers, these teenagers faced confused settlers and hostile Poles day after day. Thus they could gain the satisfaction of doing good deeds for people in need even though the real reason for their work was a racist policy of hatred, exploitation, and extermination.

The wholehearted enthusiasm of these boys and girls was easy to maintain in the early years of the war, when it seemed for a while that Germany really could conquer all Europe. Poland quickly fell to the Germans in September 1939. (The Soviet Union invaded Poland from the east that same month and took possession of the eastern third of the nation.) On April 9, 1940, Germany invaded Denmark and Norway, taking the two Scandinavian countries by surprise and conquering both within weeks. On May 10, elements of the German army and air force moved into Belgium, Holland, and Luxembourg and invaded France by going around the French defense fortification, called the Maginot Line. Two weeks later, British troops were evacuated from the European continent. On June 14, Paris, the French capital, fell to the Germans.

Hitler turned next to the British, planning to destroy the Royal Air Force. From August 1940 to May 1941, the Luftwaffe bombed British air bases and cities. But when the British could not be beaten into submission, Hitler turned east. On June 22, 1941, Germany invaded Russia, to the apparent surprise of Soviet dictator Joseph Stalin, who had considered Hitler his ally. The quick victory Hitler had expected did not happen, and German troops dressed and equipped for summer fighting faced the fiercest winter Russia had seen in fifty years.

On the home front, German children were put to work helping to bring in the harvest and to deliver draft notices. They served as air-raid wardens, making sure their neighbors followed blackout orders. When the German army at the eastern front faced the savage Russian winter of 1941, youngsters rounded up skis to send to the soldiers. They also provided guard, propaganda, messenger, and fire-fighting services; performed first aid; operated searchlights; gave emergency aid to the post office, police, and railways; did errands and other small jobs for the army; worked in factories; collected old clothes; and did welfare and cultural work.

With boys away at war or in training camps, much of this work was done by girls. During the war, young people made a huge contribution to keeping the German economy running. For example, the 1942 harvest was brought in with the help of 600,000 boys and 1.4 million girls.

Ultimately, the war meant something else for Hitler Youths: They lost their position as the pampered pets of the Third Reich and became muddy, tired soldiers like everyone else. The Hitler Youth provided the expanding Waffen-SS, the SS military branch, with its main source of recruits. The young soldiers were suicidally aggressive in battle. About 60,000 boys, some as young as seventeen, had been brought into the SS by mid-1940.

Over the next two years, the SS and the army competed with each other for the shrinking number of strong young men to fling into combat. Some parents raised objections, but to no avail. Even those young Germans who seemingly were cut off from the Fatherland were expected to return and fight. Johann, son of a German businessman and a Hitler Youth member in Kobe, Japan, remembers the difficult situation that he and his peers were left in. There were no flights from Japan to Germany, and surface travel meant crossing the Soviet Union or the Pacific Ocean—neither of which was possible during the war.

"About the only way was by submarine," he recalls. "The German navy had a base in Singapore, and once in a while submarines would come up to Japan. So a number of people that I knew were moved to Germany that way. You were not allowed to have claustrophobia. Some of them didn't make it because the submarines were attacked and sunk. Those that arrived in Germany invariably would be killed within six months."

Nazi Germany stood at the peak of its power in the fall of 1942, controlling the largest German empire in history. Hitler's conquests included most of the north and south shores of the Mediterranean, territory from the Arctic Ocean in the north to Egypt in the south, and most of Europe. That winter, however, the tide of war turned.

In North Africa, German and Italian troops were overrun by the Allies; the survivors landed in prisoner-of-war camps. But the biggest blow came at Stalingrad. More than 285,000 German soldiers had attacked the Soviet city on the Volga River in August 1942. Russian troops surrounded the city and trapped them there. Finally, on January 31, 1943, with only 91,000 men left, the leaders of the devastated German Sixth Army surrendered. Only about 6,000 of those men lived to see their homeland again.

Such failures couldn't be completely covered up with propaganda. Johann, who turned fourteen that year, remembers 1943 as a time of dawning disillusionment: "I began to realize that there was a real inconsistency between what you read in the paper about the continual withdrawal of the German army and the pep talks one received from some of the leaders. I began to realize that these people were really dishonest with us."

The war leaders weren't stopping at pep talks. Desperate to get all able-bodied Germans fighting, the SS created its Helferinnen Korps, or Female Assistance Corps, in 1943. It was promoted as the only acceptable career for a woman other than being a wife and mother. Hitler also approved creation of women's battalions, the main purpose of which was to shame the men and boys into fighting harder.

In the wake of the Stalingrad and North Africa disasters, the Hitler Youth became more important than ever. Premilitary training was stepped up. Boys, who had been using rifles since the age of ten, now learned to use the army carbine and the Luger 9-millimeter handgun. They learned to throw live hand grenades and fire bazookas at tanks, and to handle the MG-41, a machine gun that could fire a thousand rounds a minute.

In mid-1943 the 12th SS Tank Division "Hitler-Jugend" was established. Recruits were to be taken from the WELs and were supposed to be seventeen and eighteen years old. In practice, boys sixteen and even younger were also signed up. About 10,000 recruits showed up that summer at the first training camp, in Belgium. It quickly became apparent that the division was short on experience, so Hitler Youth members who were considered good leaders were sent to an SS officer training school for three months. The division was organized into infantry, tank, and artillery regiments, with other units specializing in engineering, reconnaissance, anti-tank and anti-aircraft warfare, and communications.

SS recruiting tactics became more forceful as younger and younger boys were drafted. By 1944, when adult manpower was in short supply, the SS was drawing almost all recruits from the Hitler Youth. It began drafting sixteen-year-olds, and in some areas boys of fourteen and fifteen were recruited in the spring of 1944.

Germany's military fortunes, meanwhile, were steadily worsening. Allied forces landed in Normandy, on the northern coast of France, on June 6, 1944, D-Day, and were driving east toward Germany. The Hitler-Jugend tank division headed for the Normandy battle that day. On their 70-mile (113-kilometer) march to the front, they were damaged by Allied strafing attacks. But in their first real confrontation with an Allied force, the young soldiers knocked out twenty-eight Canadian tanks; they lost only six of their own.

Hitler Youth soldiers fought ferociously. Many fought to the death rather than surrender. Within a month, twenty percent of the tank division's members had been killed, and another forty percent were missing or wounded. Half the division's tanks and armored vehicles had been lost. In September 1944, three months after its first battle, all that remained were six hundred soldiers— with no tanks and no ammunition for artillery.

The division was re-equipped and sent to fight in the Ardennes offensive of late 1944, also called the Battle of the Bulge, and was later sent to fight in Hungary. But it never really recovered.

Other Hitler Youth units were summoned to shore up Germany's defenses near the western front. The boys' primary task was to free regular troops to fight at the front. But they also had to prepare for the unthinkable possibility that the enemy would get that far into the Fatherland.

Alfons Heck, a sixteen-year-old Hitler Youth, was put in charge of about 180 boys age fifteen and older who were part of this effort. His assignment was to dig an anti-tank barrier 18 feet (5.5 meters) wide at the top, 15 feet (4.5 meters) deep, and 3 miles (5 kilometers) long. His equipment for this daunting job: shovels, picks, crowbars, and wheelbarrows. But the boys in his command were no longer children.

Younger and younger boys were pressed into
service in the closing months of the war.
This group of fifteen- and sixteen-year-olds
surrendered to U.S. troops in April 1945.

"It was astonishing," Heck later wrote, "how fast young boys matured under pressure and unrelenting duty. Most of them acted like hardened men. Many had already lost a father or brother in battle and they were inured to the possibility of death."

On September 25, 1944, Hitler issued a decree creating the Volkssturm, or People's Storm, which was to defend German soil to the last breath, foot by foot, and house by house. All males between fifteen and sixty who were not already fighting were ordered to join. Those who disobeyed or deserted could be shot, as in the regular army. The Nazi party, not the army, controlled this ragtag militia, but Hitler Youth members brought it to life and, in the end, died with it. Eleven-year-old boys were assigned to handle anti-tank weapons, and girls staffed anti-aircraft batteries.

By the end of 1944, the SS and the army suffered a serious shortage of officers. Hitler ordered that Hitler Youth boys be trained for these jobs, and recruiting focused on fifteen-year-olds. The first session began with two thousand boys in February 1945—when Germany was being pummeled by the Allies and the war's end was only months away.

Some army leaders resisted sending children to their deaths on the battlefield, and they objected to the plans of Himmler and Hitler Youth chief Artur Axmann. But most accepted the youths, especially on the eastern front, where the fighting was the fiercest and casualties were the highest. Tens of thousands of boys died fighting the Soviet Union's Red Army. Hundreds committed suicide rather than be caught alive, because they knew the Russians would show no mercy to a Hitler Youth.

Across the killing fields of Germany, younger and younger boys and girls were taking up weapons and charging to the defense of Hitler's lost cause. During the fighting for the city of Aachen, for instance, American soldiers captured armed German boys as young as eight years of age. Units of the Waffen-SS and the People's Storm that were made up entirely of fanatic Hitler Youth members suffered the worst casualties. Small bands of Hitler Youths ambushed American troops. In retaliation, the Americans mounted air strikes that leveled several villages.

Hitler Youth boys and BDM girls were also trained as spies and saboteurs in the waning days of the war. The guerrilla project, established in February 1945, was called Werewolf. Youngsters were armed with explosives and arsenic and sent behind enemy lines to wreak whatever havoc they could. Many were wiped out by Allied forces. Two boys who tried to ambush an American supply convoy were caught, tried as spies, and executed. One was seventeen, the other sixteen.

In April 1945, Axmann began transforming Hitler Youth units into tank-destroyer troops. With its military-style structure, and with hurried training at the WELs, what remained of the organization was easily turned into a combat machine. Axmann was determined to send his young charges into the carnage of battle. And, despite an order from his commanding officer forbidding this senseless sacrifice, Axmann committed his tank-destroyer troops to one final bloody battle.

The Battle of Berlin was the last gasp of Hitler's mighty war machine, and a pathetic gasp it was. Berlin had an area of 341 square miles (883 square kilometers), almost as big as New York City. Its defense was in the hands of troops ranging from fifteen-year-old Hitler Youth members to men in their seventies, derisively referred to as the "Old Bones." The 60,000 troops of the People's Storm were untrained and exhausted, and they were assigned to dig trenches around the city. One third were unarmed, and the rest carried an assortment of captured weapons and almost no usable ammunition. BDM girls, meanwhile, cared for wounded soldiers and civilians, policed the chaotic railroad stations, and helped frantic refugees.

On April 19, the day before Hitler's birthday, ten-year-old girls and boys in Berlin were ceremonially inducted into the Hitler Youth as they had been every year on that date. They were exhorted to fight for the victory of Greater Germany. The next day, there were six air raids on the city.

That day, April 20, at his last birthday celebration, Hitler called some of his young warriors to his bunker. Trembling and stoop-shouldered, the Fuehrer pinned medals on the boys and thanked them for their bravery and devotion. But he was not ready to give up the fight for Berlin. So boys as young as twelve were dressed in ill-fitting soldier costumes and sent to their doom. Five thousand Hitler Youths fought in the Battle of Berlin. Five hundred survived.

Axmann himself led a Hitler Youth battalion of a thousand fifteen- and sixteen-year-olds to fight on the west side of Berlin. They held on until April 30, when Hitler committed suicide. On May 1, Axmann deserted his boys and fled to the Alps. His predecessor, Baldur von Schirach, by then an official in Vienna, was also sending youths into battle to defend that city in April 1945. Seeing the hopelessness of it, Schirach also fled rather than die with his young charges.

On May 7, 1945, a week after Hitler's death, Germany surrendered unconditionally to the Allies. The Nazi Reich was no more. The next day, May 8, the Hitler-Jugend tank division, with 455 men and one tank, surrendered to the American Seventh Army.

Although the demise of Nazi Germany was welcomed by most of the world, many in the Hitler Youth generation were bereft. They had given their all to Hitler, dreaming of a bright future and exulting in their role in making that dream real. Now the dream was dead.

The victorious Allies split Germany into four sectors to be occupied by the United States, Great Britain, France, and the Soviet Union. Efforts were made to reeducate the Germans, many of whom were made to watch documentary films showing Nazi concentration camps and death camps. So grotesque and incomprehensible were the pictures of stacked corpses that a number of Germans dis-

A German girl is nearly overcome as she walks past the bodies of SS death camp victims. Allied forces laid out the bodies so that Germans could see the Nazi atrocities.

missed them as fakes. But some youths had to confront Nazi atrocities more directly, viewing or digging up mass graves. Still, amid widespread shortages, such concerns had to compete for people's attention with the day-to-day struggle for survival.

When the conquerors were trying to sort out who was guilty of war crimes and who had been dragged along by the Nazis, former Hitler Youth members were saved by their ages. They were written off as misguided children. "We misguided children," Alfons Heck remembers, "had been far more ruthless than our elders."

Hitler Youth leaders did not escape Allied efforts to root out war criminals, however.

Baldur von Schirach, Reich youth leader from 1933 to 1940 and supreme youth leader until 1945, surrendered a month after the war ended. The International Military Tribunal at Nuremberg in 1946 sentenced him to twenty years in prison for war crimes. He remained in Berlin's Spandau jail until 1966. Schirach, one of the few accused Nazi war criminals to have admitted his guilt, said at his trial: "I have trained this generation to believe in Hitler and to be faithful to him. The youth movement which I built up bore his name. . . . It is my guilt that I have trained youth for a man who became a murderer a million times over."

Artur Axmann, national youth leader from 1940 to 1945, was captured six months after the war, fined heavily, and imprisoned until 1949; a denazification court in 1958 fined him again. But he was not convicted of war crimes. He became a leader in the postwar national socialist underground movement.

Other Hitler Youth leaders met similar fates after the war. Some went on to become businessmen, local elected officials, or political activists. Many let their Nazi past quietly fade into history.

The victims of Adolf Hitler and the Nazi Reich were many. Millions were tortured and killed in Nazi concentration camps and death camps. Tens of millions died in the war Hitler started.

There were still other victims of Hitler who escaped with their lives but would carry forever the burden of guilt for their part in Hitler's deadly rampage. These were the youngsters of the Hitler Youth generation. They were robbed of their childhood, deprived of a normal family life, and exploited like soulless machines, even as they were pampered and exalted. These were the children of the swastika.

EPILOGUE

Even a person of particular integrity and kindliness can be induced by fanaticism to do evil, because the fanatic believes that the end justifies the means. He keeps his eyes fixed on a single goal, as if bewitched, and becomes blind and deaf to everything else.

Melita Maschmann
Account Rendered

Adolf Hitler captured the hearts of a generation of Germans. When Hitler died, his movement died with him. Or did it?

There is no organization quite like the Hitler Youth today. But remnants of Hitler's program of racial hatred and violence can be found in many countries, including the United States. American groups such as the Ku Klux Klan, the Aryan Nations, and other neo-Nazis and white supremacists practice what Hitler preached.

Some of these groups have their own youth branches. The Invisible Empire Knights of the KKK in Shelton, Connecticut, maintains a Klan Youth Corps for youngsters ten through seventeen to "teach patriotism and racial separation." A KKK group based in Oxford, New Jersey, operates a Tri-K Club and a Junior Order Klan for youths twelve to seventeen. A Minneapolis-based organization called the National Socialist Movement, which claims to have branches in thirty-two states, runs a National Socialist Junior Youth (ages nine to twelve), Youth Group (twelve to fifteen), Advanced Youth (fifteen to eighteen), and Student Union (college students). The group's aim is to promote Hitler's racial views and objectives.

The closest spiritual successors of Hitler's Nazis are the "racial" skinheads. With shaven heads, tattoos, steel-toed boots, and a virulent anger at the world, these young racists emerged in the United States in 1984, when a skinhead group calling itself Romantic Violence distributed leaflets in Chicago. By 1990, skinhead groups had cropped up in thirty-four states.

A Ku Klux Klan leader addresses a group of children at a Klan youth camp in Alabama. The Klan is one of several U.S. white supremacist groups that have promoted youth activities.

Their numbers are relatively small: a 1990 survey counted about three thousand in the United States, predominantly in the western states. They range in age from thirteen to twenty-seven, but most are between sixteen and nineteen. Their only philosophy is hate, and their signature is violence. In 1988 alone, for example, skinheads were charged with these murders:

- Portland, Oregon. On November 13, three members of a group calling itself East Side White Pride spent an evening passing out literature for a white supremacist group, White Aryan Resistance, then ambushed an Ethiopian man and beat him to death with a baseball bat. The three were viewed as heroes by their fellow skins. Two were sentenced to twenty years in prison, the other to life.
- San Jose, California. A nineteen-year-old man, drunk, stabbed a white musician to death on February 28 because the musician had dared to bring a black friend to a party. The killer pleaded guilty and was sentenced to eleven years in prison.
- Las Vegas, Nevada. Two skinheads, seventeen and eighteen years old, obsessed with satanism, wanted to kill someone just for the thrill of it. On February 9 they walked into a small store and shot the clerk in the face. She died instantly. Both were convicted of murder. One was sentenced to death, the other to life in prison without possibility of parole.

These are just a sampling. Skinheads have also been involved in attacks on people and vandalism of the property of Jews, Latinos, African Americans, homosexuals, and others in Dallas, Texas; Glendale, California; Springfield, Missouri; Cleveland, Ohio; Brookline, Massachusetts; Milwaukee, Wisconsin; Spokane, Washington, and many other cities across the United States. They paint swastikas on synagogues, wear Nazi insignias, and give stiff-armed "Heil Hitler!" salutes during the Pledge of Allegiance.

Their chosen weapons are crude: knives, bats, chains, and steel-toed boots. In the late 1980s, skins also began amassing handguns, shotguns, and assault rifles.

Since 1979, when a group called White Student Union was founded by a skinhead at the American River College in Sacramento, California, "white student union" groups have sprung up at a number of colleges and high schools.

Skinheads are mostly alienated and directionless. Many come from broken homes, and some abuse alcohol or drugs. They are also armed and dangerous. And older, established white supremacist groups have begun to recognize that the skins are a pool from which to recruit members.

The Ku Klux Klan and neo-Nazi groups such as the White Aryan Resistance and the American Front have appeared with skinheads on television talk shows, given them paramilitary training, and invited them to national white supremacist conventions. One such group calls skinheads its "front-line warriors."

And the skins, at first a collection of independent groups, have begun to form a loose national network. Some have started growing their hair and getting involved in local political activities. Skinheads have taken their own recruiting efforts to high schools in several states and have even tried to recruit elementary school students in California.

For the most part, skinheads are simply too rebellious to form an effective, centralized national organization. But what would happen if a charismatic leader came along to harness the restless, violent anger and racism of these youths? What if that leader could also tap into the fears and angers of law-abiding Americans? Is there a hidden streak of racism that might be exploited the way Hitler whipped up fear of an imaginary Jewish menace?

Perhaps one need look no further than the 1991 election for governor in Louisiana. David Duke, a former Klan leader and founder of the National Association for the Advancement of White People, polled thirty-nine percent of the vote with a thinly disguised message of racism and white supremacy. Duke lost that election. But, clearly, there is an audience in America for this sinister idea.

And here is something to consider: When Hitler joined what became the Nazi party, it was a pathetic group of fewer than a dozen social misfits. The band of roughnecks the party hired as bouncers for meetings in the early 1920s grew into the SA, the Nazi storm troopers. In the early 1990s, extremist groups like the White Aryan Resistance and the Klan were hiring young skinheads as security guards for their meetings.

And what about the indoctrination in the Hitler Youth that some have called brainwashing? The teaching of unquestioning obedience? That finds its parallel in some cults, or charismatic groups. Charismatic groups can be religious, political, commercial, or pseudotherapeutic. They can be small or large, local or international, and not all are bad. But the ones that can turn destructive have several things in common.

Destructive cults keep tight control over members for the benefit of the leader, who is often thought to have godlike powers. They demand unquestioning submission to the leader's will; promote the view that the cult is good and the outside world is bad; discourage rational, critical thinking; declare that the ends justify the means; and insist that the needs of the group come before those of any individual. Anyone who dares to pull away or express doubts is ostracized. Often, members are put on a schedule in which every minute is busy, so there is no time for free thought. They may be kept hungry or tired much of the time. Sound familiar?

Some of these cults have exploded in violence and met tragic ends. Others have managed to fit into society just enough to survive. But a crucial difference between charismatic groups in the United States and the Hitler Youth is that the cults are not an arm of the government and do not have police power.

What if one did?

Look at the reign of the Ayatollah Khomeini in Iran. In Iran's war with Iraq in the 1980s, Khomeini ordered that youths of twelve to seventeen run unarmed into battle, detonating land mines as they went to open the way for regular soldiers. Local clergy recruited youngsters for this assignment, and their families supported it, all in the name of religious commitment. In effect, the state became the charismatic group and took advantage of a tradition of self-sacrifice in the Shiite Islamic faith.

Were the young Iranians—or the young people in Hitler's Germany—insane? Or were they patriotic and willing to obey a leader they believed in, as idealistic youths anywhere might?

The children of the Hitler Youth were not told about the killing of the Jews. Although some asked questions, they usually received only vague answers. The signs of evil were there, but they gradually came to embrace the attitude that the end justifies the means. Thus they blinded themselves to things that might have weakened their worship for their one god, Hitler.

The appeal of National Socialism was that it gave young people a feeling of power, a sense that they could control their destinies and the world. In reality, they were the ones being controlled and held captive. They gave up their right to independent thought, and in a free society that is the greatest power a person can have.

NOTES

Chapter One

"Faith is harder. . . ." Adolf Hitler, *Mein Kampf*, pp. 337–338.
"This is illegal. . . ." Alfons Heck, *A Child of Hitler*, pp. 97–98.
"The nationalization of. . . ." Hitler, *Mein Kampf*, p. 338.
"a province of. . . ." William L. Shirer, *The Rise and Fall of the Third Reich*, p. 347, quoted from the so-called Anschluss law drafted by Dr. Wilhelm Stuckart.

Chapter Two

"I am beginning. . . ." Gerhard Rempel, *Hitler's Children*, pp. 1–2, quoted from Hermann Rauschning, *The Voice of Destruction*. New York: 1940.
"fighters against. . . ." Peter D. Stachura, *Nazi Youth in the Weimar Republic*, p. 7, quoted from a March 1922 proclamation in the *Voelkischer Beobachter*.

Chapter Three

"This self-confidence must. . . ." Hitler, *Mein Kampf*, p. 411.
"tough as leather. . . ." Melita Maschmann, *Account Rendered*, p. 26, quoting Hitler.
"We had meetings. . . ." Interview with the author, November 14, 1991.
"Most children. . . ." Interview with the author, November 30, 1991.
"Everybody that I. . . ." Interview with the author, November 13, 1991.
"My father was. . . ." Interview with the author, December 19, 1991.
"My parents tried. . . ." Interview with the author, November 18, 1991.

Chapter Four

"Above all we appeal. . . ." Hitler, *Mein Kampf*, p. 406.

"You, my youth. . . ." Heck, p. 22.

"Adolf Hitler. . . ." Claudia Koonz, *Mothers in the Fatherland*, pp. 286–287, quoted from Robert Waite, *Hitler: The Psychopathic God*. New York: Basic, 1977.

"What held my. . . ." Maschmann, p. 11.

"I wanted to escape. . . ." Maschmann, p. 12.

"Today Germany. . . ." H. W. Koch, *The Hitler Youth*, p. 88.

"My father came. . . ." Interview with the author, November 18, 1991.

"We dreamed then. . . ." Maschmann, pp. 218–219.

Chapter Five

"Give the German. . . ." Hitler, *Mein Kampf*, p. 546.

"In the presence. . . ." Shirer, p. 253.

Alfons Heck became. . . . Heck, p. 34.

"The goal of. . . ." Hitler, *Mein Kampf*, p. 414.

"is a subject. . . ." Hitler, *Mein Kampf*, p. 441.

"Be Faithful . . . Die Laughing!" Koonz, p. 196.

"What other peoples. . . ." Hitler, *Mein Kampf*, p. 648.

"to secure for . . . sacrifice of the people." Hitler, *Mein Kampf*, p. 652.

Chapter Six

"None of us. . . ." Heck, pp. 205–206.

"About the only. . . ." Interview with the author, December 19, 1991.

"I began to. . . ." Interview with the author, December 19, 1991.

"It was astonishing. . . ." Heck, p. 104.

"We misguided children. . . ." Heck, p. 199.

"I have trained. . . ." Joe J. Heydecker and Johannes Leeb, *The Nuremberg Trial*, p. 241.

Chapter Seven

"Even a person. . . ." Maschmann, p. 219.

SUGGESTIONS FOR FURTHER READING

The story of the Hitler Youth is one small aspect of the fascinating history of the Third Reich. For readers who would like to learn more, I especially recommend these works:

Heck, Alfons. *A Child of Hitler: Germany in the Days When God Wore a Swastika*. Frederick, Colo.: Renaissance House Publishers, 1985. The first volume of a two-part memoir (see next entry) of the Hitler Youth and Nazi Germany.

Heck, Alfons. *The Burden of Hitler's Legacy*. Frederick, Colo.: Renaissance House Publishers, 1988.

Hitler, Adolf. *Mein Kampf*. Translated by Ralph Manheim. Boston: Houghton Mifflin, 1971.

Koonz, Claudia. *Mothers in the Fatherland: Women, the Family and Nazi Politics*. New York: St. Martin's Press, 1987. A look at the oppressive demands on women in the Third Reich.

Maschmann, Melita. *Account Rendered: A Dossier on My Former Self*. Translated by Geoffrey Strachan. New York: Abelard-Schuman, 1965. An account of life in the League of German Girls by a woman who was fifteen when Hitler came to power.

Rogasky, Barbara. *Smoke and Ashes: The Story of the Holocaust*. New York: Holiday House, 1988. A brief account of the Holocaust that makes a powerful statement with statistics.

Ryan, Cornelius. *The Last Battle*. New York: Simon and Schuster, 1966. An account of the Battle of Berlin.

Shirer, William L. *The Rise and Fall of the Third Reich: A History of Nazi Germany*. New York: Simon and Schuster, 1960.

Other sources used in this book:

Breitbart, Aaron. Interview with the author, March 2, 1992.

Childs, Harwood L., trans. *The Nazi Primer: Official Handbook for Schooling the Hitler Youth*. New York: Harper & Brothers Publishers, 1938.

Galanter, Marc. *Cults: Faith, Healing, and Coercion*. New York: Oxford University Press, 1989.

Grunberger, Richard. *The 12-Year Reich: A Social History of Nazi Germany 1933–1945*. New York: Holt, Rinehart and Winston, 1971.

Heydecker, Joe J., and Leeb, Johannes. *The Nuremberg Trial*. Translated and edited by R. A. Downie. Originally published by The World Publishing Co., Cleveland, OH, 1962. Westport, CT: Greenwood Press, 1975.

Hilberg, Raul. *The Destruction of the European Jews*. Student edition. New York: Holmes & Meier, 1985.

Hitler, Adolf. *My New Order*. Collection of Hitler's speeches. Edited with commentary by Raoul de Roussy de Sales. Originally published 1941. New York: Octagon Books, 1973.

Koch, H. W. *The Hitler Youth: Origins and Development 1922–45*. New York: Stein and Day, 1975.

Langone, Michael D., and Ross, Joan Carol. *Cults: What Parents Should Know*. Weston, Mass.: American Family Foundation, 1988.

Marrin, Albert. *Hitler*. New York: Viking Kestrel, 1987.

Peukert, Detlev J. K. *Inside Nazi Germany: Conformity, Opposition, and Racism in Everyday Life*. Translated by Richard Deveson. New Haven and London: Yale University Press, 1987.

Rempel, Gerhard. *Hitler's Children: The Hitler Youth and the SS*. Chapel Hill: University of North Carolina Press, 1989.

Stachura, Peter D. *Nazi Youth in the Weimar Republic*. Santa Barbara, Calif.: Clio Books, 1975.

Stephens, Frederick J. *Hitler Youth: History, Organisation, Uniforms and Insignia*. London: Almark Publishing, 1973.

Tobias, Fritz. *The Reichstag Fire*. First American edition. Translated by Arnold J. Pomerans. New York: G. P. Putnam's Sons, 1964.

Interviews by the author with former members of the Hitler Youth and its affiliates (League of German Girls, Young Folk, Young Girls), conducted November 13, 14, 18, 30, December 19, 1991.

CHRONOLOGY

April 20, 1889	Adolf Hitler is born in Braunau am Inn, Austria.
Nov. 9, 1918	The Weimar Republic is proclaimed in Germany. Its constitution provides for democracy, equality, personal freedoms.
Nov. 11, 1918	World War I ends.
June 28, 1919	Germany signs the Treaty of Versailles.
September 1919	Hitler encounters a tiny political group called the German Workers' Party. He joins it.
April 1, 1920	The party changes its name to the National Socialist German Workers' Party, or the Nazi party.
March 1922	Hitler proclaims the formation of the first Nazi party youth group.
Nov. 8, 1923	Hitler makes a grab for power in Bavaria in what comes to be called the Beer Hall Putsch. The failed rebellion lands Hitler in prison for treason.
Dec. 20, 1924	Hitler gets out of prison. He returns to his work building the Nazi party.
Fall 1925	*Mein Kampf* is published.
July 1926	The Hitler Youth is formally founded, with Kurt Gruber as its leader.
Aug. 19–20, 1927	Gruber leads 300 youths at the Nazi party rally in Nuremberg, prompting a tribute from Hitler.
April 1929	The Hitler Youth is declared the only official youth group of the party.
July 1930	The Bund Deutscher Maedel, the League of German Girls, is formally named.
Oct. 30, 1931	Baldur von Schirach is appointed youth leader of the Nazi party.

April 13, 1932	The Weimar government bans a number of Nazi party groups, including the Hitler Youth. The ban lasts only a few months.
Jan. 30, 1933	Hitler is named chancellor of Germany.
Feb. 27, 1933	The Reichstag, the German Parliament building, burns, triggering the first burst of government-backed Nazi terror.
March 23, 1933	The Reichstag passes the Enabling Act, which gives Hitler dictatorial powers.
April 1, 1933	Hitler proclaims a boycott of Jewish shops.
May 10, 1933	Nazi book-burning begins.
June 1933	Schirach is named youth leader of the German Reich. He initiates a program of "coordination" that disbands almost all other youth groups.
Aug. 2, 1934	After President Paul von Hindenburg's death, Hitler names himself Fuehrer and Reich chancellor.
Oct. 7, 1934	The Reich Land Service is introduced, sending youths to work on farms.
Sept. 15, 1935	The Nuremberg Laws take away German citizenship from Jews and impose harsh conditions on them.
March 7, 1936	German troops reoccupy the demilitarized Rhineland.
December 1936	The Hitler Youth Law makes membership compulsory for youths ten to eighteen.
Jan. 30, 1937	Hitler proclaims the Treaty of Versailles dead.
March 13, 1938	Germany's annexation, or Anschluss, of Austria is proclaimed.
Nov. 9, 1938	The Nazis nationwide torch synagogues and vandalize Jewish homes and businesses in the "Night of Broken Glass," Kristallnacht.
March 1939	Hitler manages a bloodless takeover of Czechoslovakia.
Sept. 1, 1939	Germany invades Poland, launching World War II. Poland falls within a month.

Oct. 7, 1939	Hitler orders SS chief Heinrich Himmler to oust Polish farmers from their homes and hand the land over to transplanted Germans.
April 9, 1940	Germany invades Denmark and Norway. Both fall within weeks.
May 10, 1940	German troops invade Belgium, Holland, and Luxembourg. From there, they begin the invasion of France.
June 14, 1940	Paris falls to the Germans.
August 1940	Artur Axmann succeeds Schirach as youth leader.
August 1940 to May 1941	Germany bombs British air bases and major cities.
June 22, 1941	Germany invades Russia.
January 1942	Nazi leaders formalize their "Final Solution of the Jewish Problem" in a conference at Wannsee.
Fall and winter, 1942–43	The Allies overcome German and Italian troops in North Africa.
Jan. 31, 1943	The German Sixth Army, with only about one third of its soldiers surviving, surrenders to the Russians at Stalingrad.
June 24, 1943	Creation of the 12th SS-Panzer Division Hitler-Jugend is ordered.
June 6, 1944	D-Day; Allies land at Normandy, on the northern coast of France. The Hitler-Jugend tank division is sent to the Normandy front.
Sept. 25, 1944	Hitler creates the People's Storm to defend German soil foot by foot, house by house.
February 1945	The Werewolf project is initiated, training youngsters in guerrilla warfare.
April 20, 1945	On his 56th birthday, Hitler pins medals on some Hitler Youths in his bunker in Berlin, then sends them out to fight for the city.
April 30, 1945	Hitler commits suicide.
May 7, 1945	Germany surrenders unconditionally.
May 8, 1945	The Hitler-Jugend tank division surrenders to the American Seventh Army.

INDEX

Page numbers in *italics*
refer to illustrations.